GN01032997

Chefs' Special

Seafood Platter

Seafood Platter

Compiled by
Master Chefs
of India

Lustre Press
Roli Books

GOURMET DELIGHT

In a land so rich in cultural heritage, it is but natural that the Indian cuisine is multifarious, offering a delight to both the eye and the palate. Its myriad flavours and cooking traditions find their roots in its historical influences. The Mughals revolutionised the art of Indian cooking with their delectable *biryanis* (an exquisite oven preparation with meat/vegetables, herbs and seasonings), *kormas* (a spicy meat or vegetarian preparation), *kebabs* and *tikkas* (meat and vegetables cooked in small pieces, usually on skewers) made in a *tandoor* (an oven made of mud and heated by a slow charcoal fire). The British Raj spawned an interesting Anglo-Indian gastronomic culture which is still eaten with relish. Different regions in India offer their own specialities with their very own taste, subtlety and aroma. The country's vast reservoir of spices made from its abundance of tropical herbs, serves as garnishing and contains medicinal and preservative properties. Indeed the range of the Indian cuisine can amaze even a connoisseur.

This book offers you a *Seafood Platter* with sumptuous fare—each recipe an easy winner. Try them on the griddle, stir-fried in a pan, or baked in an oven or tandoor— pomfret, sole, fresh-water fish, prawns and shrimps . . . as snacks or meals. A few basic recipes of popular cooking ingredients, including *masalas,* Indian equivalents of foods given in each list of ingredients and a Glossary of Cooking Terms are valuable add-ons. Some chutneys, rice preparations and relishing *rotis* (pp. 88-91) serve as a complementary fillip. And to provide a finishing touch, a sprinkling of 'handy hints' are added as sure-fire remedies to common culinary problems.

BASIC INDIAN RECIPES

Green Chilli Paste
Chop the required quantity of green chillies and process until pulped.

Garam Masala (for 450 gm)
Put 200 gm cumin, 35 gm black peppercorns, 45 gm black cardamoms, 30 gm green cardamoms, 60 gm coriander seeds, 20 gm cloves, 20 gm cinnamon sticks, 15 gm bayleaves and 2 nutmegs in a processor and grind to a fine powder. Transfer to a bowl, add 20 gm mace powder and 30 gm ginger powder and mix well. Sieve and store in an airtight container.

Brown Onion Paste
Fry sliced onions over medium heat till brown. Drain excess oil and allow to cool. Process until pulped (using very little water if required). Refrigerate in an airtight container.

Yoghurt
Boil milk and keep aside till lukewarm. Add 2 tsp yoghurt to the milk and mix well. Allow to ferment for 6-8 hours.

Red Chilli Paste
Chop red chillies and process until pulped.

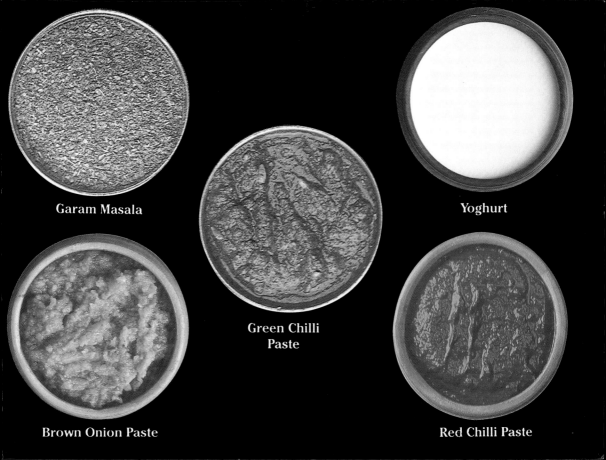

Garam Masala

Yoghurt

Green Chilli
Paste

Brown Onion Paste

Red Chilli Paste

Ginger/Garlic Paste
Soak ginger/garlic overnight. Peel, chop and process to pulp. Refrigerate in an airtight container.

Onion Paste
Peel and quarter onions and process until pulped. Refrigerate in an airtight container.

Tomato Purée
Peel, deseed and chop the tomatoes. Transfer to a pan, add 1 lt water, 8 cloves, 8 green cardamoms, 15 gm ginger, 10 gm garlic, 5 bayleaves and 5 black peppercorns and cook on medium heat till the tomatoes are tender. Cool and process to a pulp.

Cottage Cheese (*Paneer*)
Heat 3 lt milk. Just before it boils, add 60 ml/4 tsp lemon juice or white vinegar. Strain the milk through a muslin cloth and hang for 2-3 hours to drain the whey and moisture.

Khoya
Boil milk in a wok (*kadhai*). Reduce heat and cook, stirring occasionally, till the quantity is reduced to half. Then stir constantly and scrape from all sides till a thick paste-like consistency is obtained. Allow to cool. *Khoya* is also called wholemilk fudge.

Ginger-Garlic Paste

Onion Paste

Cottage Cheese

Tomato Purée

Khoya

SESAME PRAWN TIKKAS

Serves: 4-6   Preparation time: 45 minutes   Cooking time: 15 minutes

Ingredients

King prawns *(bare jhinge)* 12
Lemon juice *10 ml / 2 tsp*
Sesame seeds *(til) 30 gm / 2 tbsp*
Oil *220 ml / 1¼ cups*
Paprika (whole red chillies)
5 gm / 1 tsp
Garlic *(lasan)*, crushed *5 gm / 1 tsp*
Red chilli powder *3 gm / ½ tsp*
Turmeric *(haldi)* powder
3 gm / ½ tsp
Salt to taste
Green coriander *(hara dhaniya)*,
chopped *(optional) 5 gm / 1 tsp*

Method

1. Wash, clean and devein prawns. Pat them dry. Rub lemon juice onto the prawns and set aside.

2. Coarsely grind 1 tsp sesame seeds. Put the rest aside to be used later for frying.

3. Mix the coarsely ground sesame seeds with 1 tsp oil and the rest of the ingredients to form a marinade. Coat the prawns with this marinade, cover the dish and put aside for 30 minutes.

4. Heat oil in a frying pan till it starts smoking. Reduce fire to medium. Coat prawns evenly with the remaining sesame seeds and deep fry till they are crisp and golden brown.

5. Garnish with chopped coriander and serve hot, accompanied by chilli sauce.

PRAWN CUTLETS

Serves: 4-6   Preparation time: 30 minutes   Cooking time: 30 minutes

Ingredients

Prawns *(jhinge)* / shrimps, shelled,
chopped *400 gm / 2 cups*
Onions (medium), finely chopped *2*
Ginger *(adrak)*, chopped
15 gm / 1 tbsp
Green chillies, chopped *2*
Green coriander *(hara dhaniya)*,
chopped *15 gm / 1 tbsp*
Salt to taste
Lemon juice *5 ml / 1 tsp*
Fresh breadcrumbs *200 gm / 1 cup*
Turmeric *(haldi)* powder *2 gm / ¼ tsp*
Black pepper *(kali mirch)* powder
3 gm / ½ tsp
Egg *1*
Dried breadcrumbs *200 gm / 1 cup*
Oil for frying

Method

1. Mix together, the prawns / shrimps, onions, ginger, chillies, coriander, salt, lemon juice, fresh breadcrumbs, turmeric, black pepper and egg. Knead well.
2. Divide mixture into eight portions and shape them into flat round cutlets.
3. Dip the cutlets in dried breadcrumbs, coating them evenly and brushing off the excess.
4. Heat oil in a wok *(kadhai)* till it starts smoking. Lower cutlets gently into the oil and fry until they are golden brown, crisp and cooked through on each side.
5. Serve at once.

KESARI JHINGA

(Saffron-flavoured prawns)

Serves: 4   Preparation time: 4 hours   Cooking time: 10 minutes

Ingredients

Prawns *(jhinge)* (Grade-I) *1 kg*
Ginger-garlic *(adrak-lasan)* paste
(p. 8) *25 gm / 5 tsp*
Lemon juice *20 ml / 4 tsp*
Salt to taste
Sunflower oil *(surajmukhi ka tel)*
75 ml / 5 tbsp
Cream, fresh *200 gm / 1 cup*
Saffron *(kesar) a few strands*
White pepper *(safed mirch)* powder
30 gm / 2 tbsp
Butter *100 gm / ½ cup*

Method

1. Peel and devein the prawns. Prepare a marinade by mixing the ginger-garlic paste, lemon juice, salt and sunflower oil. Marinate the prawns in this and keep aside.

2. Mix cream with saffron and white pepper powder and add to the marinated prawns. Mix well and keep aside for 4 hours.

3. Skewer the prawns 1" apart and cook in a moderately hot oven for about 5-10 minutes.

4. Remove from the oven, baste with butter and roast again for 5-7 minutes.

5. Remove the prawns from the skewers and serve hot.

JHINGE KE SEEKH

(Prawn seekh kebabs)

Serves: 4   Preparation time: 30 minutes   Cooking time: 10-15 minutes

Ingredients

Prawns *(jhinge)*, cleaned,
deveined *1 kg*
Lemon juice *30 ml / 2 tbsp*
Ginger-garlic *(adrak-lasan)* paste
(p. 8) *45 gm / 3 tbsp*
Salt *10 gm / 2 tsp*
Green coriander *(hara dhaniya)*,
minced *240 gm / 1¼ cups*
Green chillies, minced *6*
Bengal gram *(chana)*, whole,
roasted *100 gm / ½ cup*
Turmeric *(haldi)* powder *5 gm / 1 tsp*
Black pepper *(kali mirch)* powder
10 gm / 2 tsp
Oil *60 ml / 4 tbsp*

Method

1. Apply lemon juice, ginger-garlic paste and salt on the prawns. Keep aside for 30 minutes.
2. Squeeze the prawns to remove excess water. Mix all the other ingredients into the prawns and mince the mixture.
3. Press the mixture along the length of the skewers to shape into kebabs.
4. Roast in a tandoor / oven / grill for 5-7 minutes. Remove, baste with oil and roast again for 5 minutes.
5. Remove from skewers and serve hot.

CHUTNEY FISH TIKKAS

Serves: 4-6   Preparation time: 3 hours 30 minutes   Cooking time: 15 minutes

Ingredients

Fish fillets, cleaned,
cut into cubes *1 kg*
Yoghurt *(dahi)* (p. 6), drained
60 gm / 4 tbsp
Cream *45 gm / 3 tbsp*
Garlic *(lasan)* paste (p. 8) *20 gm / 4 tsp*
Carom *(ajwain)* seeds *8 gm / 1½ tsp*
White pepper *(safed mirch)* powder
3 gm / ½ tsp
Cumin *(jeera)* powder *10 gm / 2 tsp*
Garam masala (p. 6) *15 gm / 1 tbsp*
Salt to taste
Lemon juice *30 ml / 2 tbsp*
Mint *(pudina)* chutney *135 ml / ³/4 cup*
Gram flour *(besan)* / rice flour
(chawal ka atta) 20 gm / 4 tsp
Butter / oil for basting

Method

1. Mix yoghurt with cream, garlic paste, carom seeds, white pepper, cumin powder, garam masala, salt, lemon juice, mint chutney and gram / rice flour.
2. Add fish cubes to the marinade, coat evenly and set aside for 2-3 hours.
3. Skewer fish 2 cm apart and roast in a preheated grill/tandoor/oven (175 °C / 350 °F) for 8-10 minutes. Baste with butter once, before roasting is complete.
4. Garnish with onion rings and serve hot.

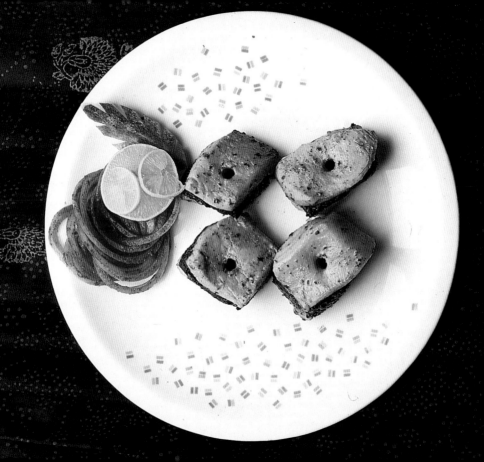

CRISPY SESAME PRAWNS

Serves: 4   Preparation time: 6 hours   Cooking time: 10-12 minutes

Ingredients

King prawns (*bare jhinge*), shelled,
deveined *1 kg*
Oil for frying
For the first marinade:
Ginger (*adrak*) paste (p. 8)
20 gm / 1 tsp
Garlic (*lasan*) paste (p. 8)
25 gm / 5 tsp
White pepper (*safed mirch*) powder
3 gm / ½ tsp
Yellow chilli powder *3 gm / ½ tsp*
Lemon juice *6 ml / 1 tsp*
For the second marinade:
Cheddar cheese, grated
60 gm / 4 tbsp
Carom (*ajwain*) seeds
15 gm / 1 tbsp

Cream *60 gm / 4 tbsp*
Green cardamom (*choti elaichi*) powder *3 gm / ½ tsp*
Mace (*javitri*) powder *3 gm / ½ tsp*
Gram flour (*besan*), roasted *45 gm / 3 tbsp*
Yoghurt (*dahi*) (p. 6), drained *120 gm / ½ cup*
Sesame seeds (*til*) *50 gm / ¼ cup*
Breadcrumbs dried,
powdered *100 gm / ½ cup*

Method

1. Mix all the ingredients of the first marinade and rub on the prawns. Keep aside for half an hour. Squeeze the prawns gently to remove excess moisture.
2. Whisk together the ingredients for the second marinade (except sesame seeds and breadcrumbs) and marinate prawns in this mixture for another 30 minutes.

3. Make a mixture of breadcrumbs and sesame seeds. Coat the prawns with the mixture and chill for 15-20 minutes.

4. Heat oil in a wok (*kadhai*) till it starts smoking. Lower heat, fry prawns for 1-2 minutes. Remove, drain and keep aside for 4-5 minutes. Deep fry again till they are crisp and golden in colour. Drain excess oil and serve hot, garnished with lemon wedges.

———— ❖ ————

Useful Substitute

Crushed cornflakes are a useful substitute for dried breadcrumbs for coating food before frying. Use them in stuffing too, in place of breadcrumbs.

———— ❖ ————

FISH TIKKAS

Serves: 4-6   Preparation time: 1 hour 30 minutes   Cooking time: 30 minutes

Ingredients

Fish fillets, cut into cubes *1 kg*
Salt to taste
Lemon juice *15 ml / 1 tbsp*
Yoghurt *(dahi)* (p. 6) *120 gm / ½ cup*
Vinegar *(sirka) 15 ml / 1 tbsp*
Garam masala (p. 6) *15 gm / 1 tbsp*
Cumin *(jeera)* seeds, ground
10 gm / 2 tsp
Carom *(ajwain)* seeds *3 gm / ½ tsp*
Red chilli powder *5 gm / 1 tsp*
Garlic *(lasan)* paste (p. 8) *10 gm / 2 tsp*
Oil / butter for basting

Method

1. Wash and dry the cubed fish fillets. Sprinkle salt and lemon juice. Set aside to marinate for half an hour.

2. In a bowl, combine yoghurt with the remaining ingredients and whisk well. Pour mixture over the fish cubes and coat evenly. Leave to marinate for at least one hour.

3. Preheat oven to 175 °C / 350 °F.

4. Roast, bake or grill till the fillets are golden brown in colour and cooked through, basting just once.

5. Serve hot.

MACHHI KOHIWADA

(Deep-fried, batter-coated fish fillets)

Serves: 4   Preparation time: 40 minutes   Cooking time: 30 minutes

Ingredients

Fish *(betki)* fillets *500 gm*
Lemon juice *30 ml / 2 tbsp*
Salt to taste
White pepper *(safed mirch)*
powder *3 gm / ½ tsp*
Ginger-garlic *(adrak-lasan)*
paste (p. 8) *100 gm / ½ cup*
Gram flour *(besan) 200 gm / 1 cup*
Cumin *(jeera)* powder *10 gm / 2 tsp*
Chaat masala *10 gm / 2 tsp*
Garam masala (p. 6) *5 gm / 1 tsp*
Red chilli paste (p. 6) *30 gm / 2 tbsp*
Green chillies, chopped *10 gm / 2 tsp*
Ginger *(adrak)*, chopped
10 gm / 2 tsp
Onions, chopped *100 gm / ½ cup*

Water as required
Oil *250 ml / 1 ¼ cup*

Method

1. Cut the fish fillets into fish fingers and marinate with lemon juice, salt, white pepper powder and ginger-garlic paste. Keep aside for 20 minutes.
2. In a bowl, mix all the other ingredients except oil. Gradually add water to make a batter of coating consistency.
3. Heat oil in a wok *(kadhai)*; dip the marinated fish fingers in the batter and deep fry until crisp and golden brown.
4. Remove, drain excess oil and serve hot.

FISH SAVOURY

Serves: 4   Preparation time: 2 hours 30 minutes   Cooking time: 30 minutes

Ingredients

Fish cut into boneless cubes *500 gm*
Oil *50 ml / 3 ²/₃ tbsp*
Green cardamoms (*choti elaichi*) *4*
Bayleaf (*tej patta*) *1*
Ginger (*adrak*) paste (p. 8)
8 gm / 1 ½ tsp
Garlic (*lasan*) paste (p.8) *8 gm / 1 ½ tsp*
Red chilli paste (p. 6) *15 gm / 1 tbsp*
Coriander (*dhaniya*) powder
15 gm / 1 tbsp
Salt to taste
Yellow chilli powder *10 gm / 2 tsp*
Poppy seed (*khus khus*) paste
10 gm / 2 tsp
Cashewnut (*kaju*) paste *20 gm / 4 tsp*
Brown onion paste (p. 6) *20 gm / 4 tsp*
Yoghurt (*dahi*) (p. 6) *250 gm / 1 ¼ cups*
Juice of lemons *2*

Method

1. Heat oil in a heavy-bottomed pan. Sauté cardamoms and bayleaf.

2. Add ginger and garlic pastes and sauté for a minute.

3. Add red chilli paste and coriander powder. Stir-fry for another minute and remove from heat.

4. Add all the other ingredients except for lemon juice, together with the fish.

5. Transfer this mixture to an oven-proof dish. Cover and seal the dish with dough.

6. Place the dish in an oven at low temperature and allow to cook for 20 minutes. Remove from the oven and sprinkle lemon juice over the fish.

7. Serve hot, accompanied by steamed rice.

SALONI FISH TIKKAS

(Fish cooked in a delightful marinade of Indian spices)

Serves: 4   Preparation time: 40 minutes   Cooking time: 15-20 minutes

Ingredients

Fish, cut into boneless pieces *800 gm*
Salt *15 gm / 1 tbsp*
White pepper (*safed mirch*) powder
5 gm / 1 tsp
Fenugreek (*methi*) powder
3 gm / ½ tsp
Turmeric (*haldi*) powder
3 gm / ½ tsp
Red chilli powder *8 gm / 1 ½ tsp*
Garam masala (p. 6) *2 gm / ⅓ tsp*
Clove (*laung*) powder *a pinch*
Ginger-garlic (*adrak-lasan*)
paste (p. 8) *25 gm / 5 tsp*
Yoghurt (*dahi*) (p. 6), drained
10 gm / 2 tsp

Vinegar (*sirka*) *150 ml / ¾ cup*
Cream *100 gm / ½ cup*
Mustard oil (*sarson ka tel*) *60 ml / 4 tbsp*
Cloves (*laung*) *16*
Charcoal piece, live *1*
Oil for basting

Method

1. Wash, clean and dry the fish pieces.
2. Prepare a marinade by mixing together salt, white pepper powder, fenugreek powder, turmeric, red chilli powder, garam masala, clove powder, ginger-garlic paste, yoghurt, vinegar and cream.
3. Marinate the fish pieces in the prepared marinade and keep aside in a bowl.

4. Make a well in the centre and put mustard oil and cloves in it. Place the live charcoal piece in the oil and cover the bowl with a lid. Seal the lid so that the smoke does not escape. Keep aside for 30 minutes.
5. Remove the lid, skewer the fish pieces and roast in a medium hot tandoor/oven/ grill for 5-6 minutes. Remove and allow excess liquids to drip off.
6. Baste with oil and roast again for 2 minutes until done. Remove from skewers and transfer to a serving platter.
7. Serve hot, accompanied by a green salad.

——— ❖ ———
Instant Chutney

Mix 1 tsp mango powder (amchur) with ¼ tsp cumin (jeera) powder, 3 tsp sugar, ½ cup water and boil for 2-5 minutes on low heat.

——— ❖ ———

FRIED FISH

Serves: 4-6   Preparation time: 1 hour 30 minutes   Cooking time: 30 minutes

Ingredients

Fish fillets *8*
Salt to taste
Black pepper *(kali mirch)* powder
5 gm /1 tsp
Lemon juice *15 ml / 1 tbsp*
Gram flour *(besan) 75 gm / 5 tbsp*
Rice flour *(chawal ka atta)*
25 gm / 5 tsp
Turmeric *(haldi)* powder *3 gm / ½ tsp*
Red chilli powder *5 gm / 1 tsp*
Cold water *100 ml / ½ cup*
Oil for deep frying
Chaat masala *a pinch*

Method

1. Cut each fillet in half and sprinkle salt, pepper and lemon juice all over. Set aside to marinate for an hour.
2. Combine the gram flour, rice flour, turmeric powder and chilli powder in a bowl. Stir in the water to form a smooth batter.
3. Heat oil in a wok *(kadhai)* till it starts smoking. Dip each piece of fish in the batter and lower into the oil.
4. Fry until crisp and golden brown on both sides. Remove and drain all excess oil.
5. Sprinkle chaat masala and serve hot, garnished with lemon wedges.

GARLIC PRAWN KEBABS

Serves: 4   Preparation time: 2 hours 30 minutes   Cooking time: 8-10 minutes

Ingredients

Prawns (*jhinge*) (jumbo), shelled,
deveined *1 kg*
Garlic (*lasan*) paste (p. 8)
15 gm / 1 tbsp
Green chilli paste (p. 6) *10 gm / 2 tsp*
Vinegar (*sirka*) *30 ml / 2 tbsp*
Salt to taste
Cornflour (*makkai ka atta*)
15 gm / 1 tbsp
Butter for basting
Poppy seeds (*khus khus*)
15 gm / 1 tbsp

Method

1. Marinate prawns in garlic and chilli pastes, vinegar and salt for 2 hours.
2. Mix in cornflour. Skewer prawns 5 cm apart and roast on low flame, basting with butter, till crisp and golden on all sides. Coat with poppy seeds (optional) and serve hot.

MAHI TIKKAS

(Fish tikkas)

Serves: 4   Preparation time: 2 hours 30 minutes   Cooking time: 15-20 minutes

Ingredients

Fish, cut into boneless pieces *1 kg*
Clarified butter *(ghee) 100 gm / ½ cup*
Onions, sliced *120 gm / ½ cup*
Garlic *(lasan)*, chopped *45 gm / 3 tbsp*
Salt to taste
Red chilli powder *30 gm / 2 tbsp*
Coriander *(dhaniya)* powder
30 gm / 2 tbsp
Cumin *(jeera)* powder *5 gm / 1 tsp*
Turmeric *(haldi)* powder
5 gm / 1 tsp
Yoghurt *(dahi)*, (p. 6) *100 gm / ½ cup*
Butter for basting

Method

1. In a pan, heat clarified butter and fry the onions till brown. Remove, drain excess clarified butter and blend to make a paste.
2. In the same pan, fry the garlic and keep aside.
3. Allow the clarified butter to cool. Mix the onion paste, garlic, all the other ingredients and the fish pieces with the clarified butter and keep aside for 2 hours.
4. Skewer the fish pieces and roast in a tandoor/oven/ grill for 5-10 minutes. Remove, baste with butter and cook further for 3-5 minutes.
5. Remove from skewers and serve hot.

TANDOORI FISH GULNAR

(Carom-flavoured tandoori fish)

Serves: 4-5   Preparation time: 1 hour 30 minutes   Cooking time: 15 minutes

Ingredients

Fish (pomfret / sole / betki),
450 gm each *4*
Malt vinegar (*sirka*) *120 ml / 2/3 cup*
Lemon juice *40 ml / 2 tbsp*
Garlic (*lasan*) paste (p. 8) *20 gm / 4 tsp*
Red chilli powder *4 gm / 3/4 tsp*
Salt to taste
Yoghurt (*dahi*) (p. 6), hung
20 gm / 4 tsp
Egg, beaten *1*
Cream *40 gm / 2 tbsp*
Ginger (*adrak*) paste (p. 8)
10 gm / 2 tsp
Gram flour (*besan*) *25 gm / 5 tsp*
Turmeric (*haldi*) powder *4 gm / 3/4 tsp*

White pepper (*safed mirch*) powder *3 gm / 2/3 tsp*
Butter for basting *50 gm / 1/4 cup*
Carom (*ajwain*) seeds *10 gm / 2 tsp*

Method

1. Wash and clean the fish. Make 3 incisions on each.
2. Marinate fish in vinegar, lemon juice, half the garlic paste, half the chilli powder and salt for half an hour.
3. Whisk yoghurt and add the remaining ingredients.
4. Remove the fish from the first marinade and marinate in the second mixture for at least 1 hour.
5. Skewer the fish from mouth to tail 2 cm apart and bake / grill for about 8 minutes.
6. Remove and hang the skewer to allow excess moisture to drip off. Baste with butter and roast or grill for a further 3 minutes. Serve hot.

JHINGA JALFREZI

(Sautéd prawn delicacy)

Serves: 4   Preparation time: 30 minutes   Cooking time: 10 minutes

Ingredients

Prawns (*jhinge*) (Grade-IV) *1 kg*
Salt to taste
Lemon juice *20 ml / 4 tsp*
Turmeric (*haldi*) powder *5 gm / 1 tsp*
Red chilli powder *15 gm / 1 tbsp*
Oil *125 ml / ½ cup*
Ginger (*adrak*), julienned (long, thin strips) *30 gm / 2 tbsp*
Garlic (*lasan*), chopped *20 gm / 4 tsp*
Onions, chopped *250 gm / 1 ¼ cups*
Tomatoes, chopped *300 gm 1 ½ cups*
Cumin (*jeera*) powder *5 gm / 1 tsp*
Tomatoes, cut into cubes
150 gm / ¾ cup
Capsicums, cut into cubes
150 gm / ¾ cups
Onions, cut into cubes *150 gm / ¾ cup*
Green coriander (*hara dhaniya*), chopped *10 gm / 2 tsp*

Method

1. Clean the prawns and marinate in a mixture of salt, lemon juice, half the turmeric powder and red chilli powder. Sauté for 2-3 minutes.

2. Heat oil in a pan. Add ginger and garlic; sauté for a minute. Add onions and sauté further till light brown.

3. Add chopped tomatoes, cumin powder and remaining turmeric and red chilli powder.

4. Stir in the prawns and cook until three-fourths done. Add tomatoes, capsicums and onions. Mix well and cook further until the prawns are done.

5. Remove from heat and serve hot, garnished with green coriander.

PICKLED PRAWNS

Serves: 4   Preparation time: 30 minutes   Cooking time: 25-30 minutes

Ingredients

Prawns (*jhinge*) (medium sized),
peeled *600 gm*
Ginger-garlic (*adrak-lasan*) paste
(p. 8) *100 gm / ½ cup*
Salt to taste
Lemon juice *45 ml / 3 tbsp*
Mustard oil (*sarson ka tel*) for frying
Onion seeds (*kalonji*) *2 gm / ½ tsp*
Mustard (*rai*) seeds *2 gm / ½ tsp*
Fenugreek (*methi*) seeds *2 gm / ½ tsp*
Whole red chillies *4*
Coriander (*dhaniya*) seeds *a pinch*
Onions, sliced *150 gm / ¾ cup*
Tomatoes, chopped *100 gm / ½ cup*
Green chillies, chopped *5 gm / 1 tsp*
Coriander (*dhaniya*) powder *a pinch*
Red chilli powder to taste
Cumin (*jeera*) powder *2 gm / ½ tsp*

Garam masala (p. 6) *2 gm / ½ tsp*
Turmeric (*haldi*) powder *2 gm / ½ tsp*
Ginger (*adrak*), julienned (long, thin strips) *10 gm / 2 tsp*
Green coriander (*hara dhaniya*), chopped *25 gm / 5 tsp*

Method

1. Mix half the ginger-garlic paste, salt and lemon juice. Marinate prawns in this mixture for half an hour.
2. Heat mustard oil in a wok (*kadhai*). Add the whole spices and sauté. Add onions and sauté till transparent. Add tomatoes, green chillies and half the coriander powder. Stir-fry for 5-10 minutes.
3. Stir in salt to taste, red chilli, coriander and cumin powders, garam masala and turmeric. Stir-fry for another 5-10 minutes. Add prawns and stir-fry till cooked. Serve, garnished with ginger and coriander.

TAWA MACHHI

(Stir-fried fish cooked on a griddle)

Serves: 4   Preparation time: 1 hour   Cooking time: 10 minutes

Ingredients

Fish, cut into boneless pieces *1 kg*
Clarified butter (*ghee*) *100 gm / ½ cup*
Carom (*ajwain*) seeds *5 gm / 1 tsp*
Onions, chopped *100 gm / ½ cup*
Ginger (*adrak*), chopped *10 gm / 2 tsp*
Green chillies, chopped *4*
Red chilli powder *5 gm / 1 tsp*
Coriander (*dhaniya*) powder
5 gm / 1 tsp
For the gravy:
Clarified butter (*ghee*) *60 gm / ¼ cup*
Garlic (*lasan*) paste (p. 8) *20 gm / 4 tsp*
Coriander (*dhaniya*) powder
10 gm / 2 tsp
Red chilli powder *5 gm / 1 tsp*
Green chillies, chopped *4*

Ginger (*adrak*), julienned (long, thin strips) *30 gm / 2 tbsp*
Tomatoes, julienned (*long, thin strips*) *100 gm / ½ cup*
Dry fenugreek (*kasoori methi*) powder *5 gm / 1 tsp*
Salt to taste
Tomatoes, chopped *500 gm / 2 ½ cups*
Garam masala (p. 6) *5 gm / 1 tsp*
Green coriander (*hara dhaniya*), chopped *20 gm / 4 tsp*

Method

1. For the gravy, heat clarified butter in a wok *(kadhai)*. Add garlic paste and sauté for a few minutes.
2. Add all the other ingredients for the gravy except garam masala and green coriander and cook till the gravy thickens. Remove from heat and keep aside.
3. Heat clarified butter on a griddle *(tawa)*. Add the

fish pieces and sauté till half done. Remove the fish pieces to the sides of the griddle.

4. Add carom seeds and sauté. Add onions along with all the ingredients and the fried fish. Stir-fry for a few minutes. Stir in the gravy and cook till the gravy dries.

5. Sprinkle garam masala and green coriander. Remove from heat and serve hot.

Chilli-Ginger Pickle

Chop green chillies and ginger into small pieces and store them in a bottle of salted lime juice. Refrigerate for a few days. The pickle will keep for a long time.

FISH FILLETS IN A SPICED MARINADE

Serves: 4-5   Preparation time: 2-4 hours   Cooking time: 15 minutes

Ingredients

Fish (steaks / fillets), with
or without bones *1 kg*
Salt for seasoning
White vinegar (*sirka*) *50 ml / ¼ cup*
Carom (*ajwain*) seeds *10 gm / 2 tsp*
Gram flour (*besan*) / flour (*maida*)
120 gm / ²/₃ cup
Red chilli powder *8 gm / 1 ²/₃ tsp*
Turmeric (*haldi*) *powder 8 gm / 1²/₃ tsp*
White pepper (*safed mirch*) powder
8 gm / 1 ²/₃ tsp
Ginger (*adrak*) paste (p. 8)
60 gm / 4 tbsp
Garlic (*lasan*) paste (p. 8)
60 gm / 4 tbsp
Lemon juice *50 ml / 4 tbsp*
Oil *200 ml / 1 cup*
Chaat masala *6 gm / 1 ¹/₃ tsp*

Method

1. Clean, wash and dry the fish.

2. Prick each piece of fish with a sharp fork.

3. Marinate the fish with salt and two-thirds of the vinegar and keep aside for 1-2 hours.

4. In a bowl, mix the dry ingredients with the ginger and garlic pastes, lemon juice and remaining vinegar and salt. Whisk to a smooth and creamy batter.

5. Coat each piece of fish evenly with the batter.

6. Arrange the fillets / steaks on a flat tray and keep aside for 1-2 hours at room temperature.

7. Heat oil in a heavy-bottomed pan. Shallow fry the fish on medium heat till crisp and golden.

8. Drain excess oil on a kitchen towel and sprinkle chaat masala.

9. Serve hot, garnished with slices of cucumber, tomato and lemon wedges.

TANDOORI POMFRET

Serves: 4   Preparation time: 3 hours 30 minutes   Cooking time: 12-15 minutes

Ingredients

Pomfrets (450 gm each) *4*
Yoghurt (*dahi*) (p. 6), drained
60 gm / 4 tbsp
Eggs, yolks *2*
Cream *45 gm / 3 tbsp*
Ginger (*adrak*) paste (p. 8)
15 gm / 3 ½ tsp
Garlic (*lasan*) paste (p. 8) 15 gm / 3 tsp
Carom (*ajwain*) seeds *10 gm / 2 tsp*
White pepper (*safed mirch*) powder
5 gm / 1 tsp
Red chilli powder *10 gm / 2 tsp*
Turmeric (*haldi*) powder *5 gm / 1 tsp*
Cumin (*jeera*) powder *10 gm / 2 tsp*
Gram flour (*besan*) *30 gm / 2 tbsp*
Lemon juice *30 ml / 2 tbsp*
Butter / oil for basting

Method

1. Clean and wash the fish. Make 2-3 incisions on both sides.
2. Whisk together the yoghurt and egg yolks with the remaining ingredients to make a smooth paste.
3. Coat the fish evenly with the yoghurt paste and leave to marinate for at least 3 hours.
4. Preheat oven to 175 °C / 350 °F. Skewer the fish from mouth to tail. Roast for 10 minutes. Remove from heat and hang the skewers to drain excess liquid. Baste with butter and roast again for 3-5 minutes.
5. Serve at once, accompanied by a salad.

FISH FILLETS IN COCONUT SAUCE

Serves: 4   Preparation time: 10-15 minutes   Cooking time: 30-40 minutes

Ingredients

Fish fillets (sole / plain), cut into 3
pieces each *4*
Oil *30 ml / 2 tbsp*
Onion seeds (*kalonji*) *5 gm / 1 tsp*
Red chillies, whole, dried *4*
Garlic (*lasan*) cloves, sliced *3*
Onion (medium), sliced *1*
Tomatoes (medium), sliced *2*
Coconut (*nariyal*), shredded
30 gm / 2 tbsp
Salt to taste
Coriander (*dhaniya*) powder
5 gm / 1 tsp
Water *150 ml / ¾ cup*
Lime juice *15 ml / 1 tbsp*
Green coriander (*hara dhaniya*),
chopped *15 gm / 1 tbsp*

Method

1. Heat oil in a wok (*kadhai*). Reduce heat and add onion seeds, dried red chillies, garlic and onion. Stir-fry for 3-4 minutes.

2. Mix in the tomatoes, shredded coconut, salt and coriander powder.

3. Add the fish pieces to the mixture and turn gently to cook evenly. Simmer and cook for 5-7 minutes.

4. Stir in the water, lime juice and chopped coriander. Cook further for 3-5 minutes or until the water evaporates.

5. Remove to a serving dish and serve hot.

SHREDDED, STIR-FRIED POMFRETS

Serves: 4-6   Preparation time: 20 minutes   Cooking time: 25 minutes

Ingredients

Pomfrets (medium-sized),
washed, shredded *2*
Oil for frying *60 ml / 4 tbsp*
Ginger (*adrak*) paste (p. 8) 5 gm / 1 tsp
Garlic (*lasan*) paste (p. 8) 5 gm / 1 tsp
Onions (medium), finely chopped *2*
Green chillies, sliced *4*
Coconut (*nariyal*) fresh, grated *400
gm / 2 cups*
Coriander (*dhaniya*) leaves
30 gm / 2 tbsp
Turmeric (*haldi*) powder 5 gm / 1 tsp
Lemon juice *15 ml / 1 tbsp*
Salt to taste
Vinegar (*sirka*) *15 ml / 1 tbsp*

Method

1. Heat oil in a pan. Add ginger and garlic pastes and sauté till brown.

2. Add onions and green chillies. Fry till brown.

3. Add coconut, coriander leaves, turmeric powder, lemon juice, vinegar and salt. Cook on slow fire for 5 minutes.

4. Add fish and stir gently till the fish is done. Serve hot.

FENNEL-FLAVOURED PRAWNS

Serves: 4   Preparation time: 25 minutes   Cooking time: 35-40 minutes

Ingredients

Prawns (*jhinge*), deveined, shelled *12*
Butter *20 gm / 4 tsp*
Fennel *(saunf)* seeds
broiled, pounded *10 gm / 2 tsp*
Garlic (*lasan*), chopped *10 gm / 2 tsp*
Green chillies, deseeded, chopped *5*
Onion paste (p. 8) *30 gm / 2 tbsp*
Lemon juice *30 ml / 2 tbsp*
Salt to taste
Fennel *(saunf)*, chopped *25 gm / 5 tsp*
Cream *100 gm / ½ cup*
Yoghurt (*dahi*) (p. 6) *100 gm / ½ cup*
Ginger (*adrak*), chopped *5 gm / 1 tsp*

Method

1. Heat butter in a pan and sauté the fennel seeds for a few seconds.

2. Add garlic, green chillies and onion paste. Stir-fry for a few minutes.

3. Mix in all the other ingredients and cook for 5-10 minutes. Remove from heat.

4. Place the prawns in an oven-proof dish; pour the prepared mixture on top. Cover the dish tightly and cook in a preheated (175 °C / 350 °F) oven for 15-20 minutes.

5. Remove from the oven. Transfer into a serving platter and serve immediately accompanied by steamed rice.

FISH FILLETS FLAVOURED WITH MUSTARD

Serves: 4-6   Preparation time: 2 hours 30 minutes   Cooking time: 20 minutes

Ingredients

Fish fillets *600 gm*
Mustard (*rai*) paste *15 gm / 1 tbsp*
Red chillies, crushed *10 gm / 2 tsp*
Salt to taste
Tomato paste *25 gm / 5 tsp*
Lemon juice *30 ml / 2 tbsp*
Onions, chopped *2*
Garlic cloves, chopped *6*
Oil *60 ml / 4 tbsp*

Method

1. Mix together the mustard paste, red chillies, salt, tomato paste and lemon juice. Marinate the fish fillets in this mixture for 2 hours.

2. Heat oil in a heavy-bottomed pan, sauté onions and garlic until transparent.

3. Gently place the fillets in the pan and cook, turning frequently, so that both the sides are evenly browned. Pour the remaining marinade along with half a cup of water over the fillets.

4. Cover the pan and simmer for 10 minutes.

5. Remove and serve hot, garnished with chopped coriander and accompanied by any Indian bread of choice (pp. 88-91).

TANDOORI SALMON

(Dill-flavoured exotic salmon)

Serves: 4   Preparation time: 1 hour   Cooking time: 15 minutes

Ingredients

Salmon (cut into ½" cubes) *1 kg*
Lemon juice *50 ml / 3 tbsp*
Salt to taste
Black pepper (*kali mirch*) powder
2 tsp / 10 gm
Yoghurt (*dahi*) (p. 6), drained
200 gm / 1 cup
Garlic (*lasan*) paste (p. 8)
20 gm / 4 tsp
Green chillies, deseeded, chopped *5*
Dill (*sooay*), chopped *10 gm / 2 tsp*
Olive oil *60 ml / 4 tsp*

Method

1. Marinate salmon cubes in lemon juice, salt and black pepper powder. Keep aside for 45 minutes.
2. Whisk yoghurt in a bowl. Add garlic paste, chopped green chillies, dill, olive oil and salt.
3. Drain salmon cubes from the first marinade and mix into the yoghurt mixture. Keep in a cool place for an hour.
4. Roast in a moderately hot tandoor or preheated oven (175 °C / 350 °F) for 10 minutes. Baste with olive oil and cook again for 2 minutes.
5. Serve with onion rings.

SHRIMPS IN COCONUT

Serves: 3-4   Preparation time: 25 minutes   Cooking time: 40-50 minutes

Ingredients

Shrimps, peeled *600 gm*
Oil *80 ml / 5 1/3 tbsp*
Mustard *(rai)* seeds *3 gm / 1/2 tsp*
Curry leaves (*meethi neem ke patte*) *2*
Garlic (*lasan*), slivered *10 gm / 2 tsp*
Onions, chopped *4*
Green chilli, chopped *1*
Coriander (*dhaniya*) powder *6 gm / 1 tsp*
Red chilli powder *5 gm / 1 tsp*
Turmeric (*haldi*) powder *3 gm / 1/2 tsp*
Coconut, fresh, grated *1*
Cumin (*jeera*), whole *10 gm / 2 tsp*
Salt to taste
Coconut (*nariyal*) milk *200 ml / 1 cup*

Method

1. Heat oil in a wok (*kadhai*). Sauté mustard seeds till they crackle. Add curry leaves, garlic slivers and chopped onions. Stir-fry till the onions are transparent.
2. Stir in all the other ingredients except coconut milk. Cook till the oil separates and appears on the surface. Add water as and when necessary to cook the curry.
3. Add the coconut milk along with the shrimps. Stir-fry till the shrimps are cooked and the curry has thickened. Remove from heat.
4. Serve hot, accompanied by a *roti* of your choice (pp. 88-91).

STUFFED TANDOORI FISH

Serves: 4   Preparation time: 3 hours 30 minutes   Cooking time: 20 minutes

Ingredients

River or sea fish (with single
central bone), 400 gm each *5*
Malt vinegar (*sirka*) *45 ml / 3 tbsp*
Salt to taste
Black pepper (*kali mirch*) powder
10 gm / 2 tsp
Fennel seeds (*saunf*) *10 gm / 2 tsp*
Ginger-garlic (*lasan-lasan*) paste
(p. 8) *50 gm / ¼ cup*
Clarified butter *(ghee) 50 gm / 3 ¹/₃ tbsp*
Gram flour (*besan*) *40 gm / 2 ²/₃ tbsp*
Lemon juice *25 ml / 5 tsp*
Red chilli powder *20 gm / 4 tsp*
Turmeric (*haldi*) powder *10 gm / 2 tsp*
Yoghurt (*dahi*) (p. 6), drained
200 gm / 1 cup
Butter to baste *50 gm / 3 ¹/₃ tbsp*

Method

1. Marinate the fish in vinegar and half the salt.
2. In a bowl, combine all the remaining ingredients and mix to a fine paste.
3. Rub the paste inside and outside the fish and let it stand for 2-3 hours.
4. Preheat the oven to 175 °C / 350 °F.
5. Skewer the fish from tail to mouth, 4 cm apart.
6. Roast in the oven for 12-15 minutes. Keep a tray underneath to collect the drippings.
7. Baste with butter. Remove and hang the skewers and let the excess moisture drip off.
8. Garnish with sliced cucumbers, tomatoes and onions.

TOMATO FISH

Serves: 4   Preparation time: 30 minutes   Cooking time: 20-25 minutes

Ingredients

Fish fillets (firm, white),
deboned, cubed *1 kg*
Turmeric (*haldi*) powder *10 gm / 2 tsp*
Salt to taste
Oil *50 ml / ¼ cup*
Onions (medium), sliced *2*
Red chilli powder *5 gm / 1 tsp*
Sugar *5 gm / 1 tsp*
Garam masala (p. 6) *10 gm / 2 tsp*
Coriander (*dhaniya*) powder
15 gm / 1 tbsp
Tomatoes, blanched, deseeded,
chopped *½ kg / 2 ½ cups*
Sour cream *30 gm / 2 tbsp*
Lemon juice *15 ml / 1 tbsp*
Green chillies, slit in half, deseeded *4*

Method

1. Marinate the fish cubes with 1½ tsp turmeric powder and salt to taste. Set aside.

2. Heat oil in a deep pan, fry the fish cubes until they are evenly browned. Put aside on a plate.

3. Add onions and sauté till transparent. Stir in red chilli powder, sugar, garam masala, coriander powder and the remaining turmeric powder. Cook for 2 minutes.

4. Add tomatoes, sour cream, lemon juice and green chillies. Bring to a boil, stirring continuously.

5. Add the fried fish cubes to the sauce and coat evenly. Simmer for 10 minutes or until the fish is cooked.

6. Serve hot, accompanied by any Indian bread (pp. 88-91).

TANDOORI LOBSTERS

Serves: 4-5   Preparation time: 5 hours   Cooking time: 10 minutes

Ingredients

Lobsters (medium) *4*
Ginger (*adrak*) paste (p. 8)
20 gm / 4 tsp
Garlic (*lasan*) paste (p. 8) *20 gm / 4 tsp*
Carom *(ajwain)* seeds *3 gm / ½ tsp*
Malt vinegar (*sirka*) *120 ml / ½ cup*
Salt to taste
Yoghurt (*dahi*) (p. 6), drained
200 gm / 1 cup
White pepper (*safed mirch*) powder
5 gm / 1 tsp
Garam masala (p. 6) *10 gm / 2 tsp*
Egg *1*
Cottage cheese (*paneer*) (p. 8)
60 gm / 4 tbsp
Gram flour *(besan)* *45 gm / 3 tbsp*
Mustard oil (*sarson ka tel*)
50 ml / 4 tbsp

Red chilli paste (p. 6) *5 gm / 1 tsp*
Butter for basting *100 gm / ½ cup*

Method

1. Cut each lobster-shell into half, then shell and devein the lobster. Wash and dry the shells and dip them in hot oil. Drain and keep aside.
2. Marinate lobsters in ginger and garlic pastes, carom seeds, vinegar and salt for 1 hour.
3. Whisk yoghurt in a large bowl. Add the remaining ingredients; coat the lobsters, keep aside for 3 hours.
4. Skewer the lobsters 2 cm apart. Keep a tray underneath to collect the excess drippings. Roast in a medium-hot tandoor / oven for 5 minutes.
5. Baste with butter and roast again for 2 minutes.
6. Place the lobster in the shell; garnish with lettuce, tomato slices and onion rings. Serve hot.

FENUGREEK-FLAVOURED PRAWNS

Serves: 4   Preparation time: 40 minutes   Cooking time: 10 minutes

Ingredients

Prawns (*jhinge*), shelled, deveined
1 ½ kg
Vinegar (*sirka*) *45 ml / 3 tbsp*
Salt to taste
Lemon juice *20 ml / 4 tsp*
Yoghurt (*dahi*) (p. 6)
240 gm / 1 ⅓ cups
Cream *200 gm / 1 cup*
White pepper (*safed mirch*) powder
8 gm / 1 ½ tsp
Cheese, grated *75 gm / 5 tbsp*
Dry fenugreek (*kasoori methi*)
powder *5 gm / 1 tsp*
Ginger-garlic (*adrak-lasan*) paste
(p. 8) *45 gm / 3 tbsp*
Garam masala (p. 6) *8 gm / 1 ½ tsp*
Saffron (*kesar*) *a few strands*
Butter for basting

Method

1. Wash the prawns with vinegar and salt water. Drain and pat dry.

2. Prepare a marinade by mixing together all the ingredients except butter.

3. Marinate the prawns in this mixture and keep aside for 30 minutes.

4. Skewer the prawns and roast in a moderately hot tandoor / oven / grill for 6-8 minutes. Remove and allow excess liquids to drip.

5. Baste lightly with butter and roast again for 2-3 minutes.

6. Remove from skewers and serve hot.

PRAWN EXOTICA

Serves: 4-6   Preparation time: 2 hours 30 minutes   Cooking time: 30 minutes

Ingredients

Prawns (*jhinge*), shelled, deveined
800 gm
Oil *60 ml / ¹/₃ cup*
Mustard *(rai)* seeds *3 gm / ½ tsp*
Green cardamoms (*choti elaichi*) *4*
Mace (*javitri*) *4*
Onions, chopped *3*
Garlic (*lasan*), *10 gm / 2 tsp*
Ginger (*adrak*), julienned (long, thin
strips) *10 gm / 2 tsp*
Green chillies, slit *2*
Salt to taste
Curry leaves (*meethi neem
ke patte*) *2*
Cream *300 gm / 1 ½ cups*

Method

1. Heat oil in a non-stick pan. Add mustard seeds, cardamoms and mace and sauté till they crackle.
2. Add chopped onions, garlic, ginger and slit green chillies. Cook till the onions are soft. Add salt.
3. Place the prawns in an oven-proof dish and pour the prepared mixture on top.
4. Add the curry leaves and cream to the mixture.
5. Seal the dish with aluminium foil and cook in a preheated oven (175 °C / 350 °F) for 25 minutes.
6. Remove from oven; garnish with chopped coriander and serve hot, accompanied by any Indian bread (pp. 88-91).

ZAFRANI MAHI KEBABS

(Fish patties flavoured with sesame seeds)

Serves: 4-5　Preparation time: 45 minutes　Cooking time: 15 minutes

Ingredients

Fish (white), boneless *900 gm*
Chaat masala *5 gm / 1 tsp*
Cream *30 gm / 2 tbsp*
Egg, white *1*
Eggs, beaten *3*
Garam masala (p. 6) *5 gm / 1 tsp*
Garlic (*lasan*) paste *40 gm / 2 ²/₃ tbsp*
Ginger (*adrak*) paste *40 gm / 2 ²/₃ tbsp*
Gram flour (*besan*) / flour (*maida*)
60 gm / 4 tbsp
Green chillies, chopped *6 gm / 1 tsp*
Green coriander (*hara dhaniya*),
chopped *10 gm / 2 tsp*
Lemon juice *45 ml / 3 tbsp*
Mace (*javitri*) powder *3 gm / ²/₃ tsp*

Oil for frying *200 ml / 1 cup*
Saffron (*kesar*) *2 gm / ¹/₂ tsp*
Salt to taste
Vetivier (*kewda*) *3 drops*
White pepper (*safed mirch*) powder *5 gm / 1 tsp*
Yellow chilli (*deghi mirch*) powder *6 gm / 1 ¹/₃ tsp*
Sesame seeds (*til*) *60 gm / 4 tbsp*

Method

1. Boil the fish. Debone and mince well.
2. In a bowl, mix all the ingredients, except the sesame seeds and egg white, with the minced fish.
3. Divide the mixture into 20 equal portions and shape into round balls. Press each ball between the palms to make a patty, approximately 6 cm in diameter.

4. Beat the egg white lightly.

5. Coat each patty with the egg white and sprinkle sesame seeds evenly on top.

6. Heat the oil and shallow fry each patty until golden.

7. Arrange the patties on a serving platter and sprinkle chaat masala. Serve with sliced cucumbers, tomatoes and lemon wedges.

———— ❖ ————

Oil(less) Food!

If you're health conscious and worried about extra oil in your food, don't worry! After cooking a dish, refrigerate it and remove the solidified fat before reheating it.

———— ❖ ————

PATRANI MACHHI

(Low-fat, chutney-flavoured fish)

Serves: 4-5   Preparation time: 45 minutes   Cooking time: 15 minutes

Ingredients

Fish fillets *1 kg*
Banana leaves or aluminium foil
Lemon juice *25 ml / 5 tsp*
Oil *30 ml / 2 tbsp*
Salt to taste
Malt vinegar (*sirka*) *90 ml / 1/3 cup*
For the green coconut chutney:
Coriander (*dhaniya*) seeds
50 gm / 1/4 cup
Cumin (*jeera*) seeds *15 gm / 3 tsp*
Fresh coconut (*nariyal*), grated
100 gm / 1/2 cup
Garlic (*lasan*) *20 gm / 4 tsp*
Green chillies *6*
Green coriander (*hara dhaniya*),
chopped *15 gm / 3 tsp*
Red chilli powder *5 gm / 1 tsp*
Sugar *25 gm / 5 tsp*

Method

1. Marinate the fish fillets in vinegar, lemon juice and salt for 30 minutes.
2. Trim, wash and wipe the banana leaves.
3. Blend all the ingredients for the green chutney with a little water in a blender to make a fine paste.
4. Apply this paste liberally on the fish fillets.
5. Oil the banana leaves and wrap each fillet separately in them. Alternately, wrap each fillet in foil.
6. Steam the fish in a steamer for 10-15 minutes.
7. Unwrap the fish, arrange on a platter and serve, garnished with lemon wedges.

BALTI POMFRET

(Stir-fried pomfret in spicy mixture)

Serves: 4   Preparation time: 30 minutes   Cooking time: 10 minutes

Ingredients

Pomfret fillets *800 gm*
Salt to taste
Malt vinegar (*sirka*) *60 ml / 3 tbsp*
Tamarind (*imli*) *50 gm / 3 tbsp*
Red chilli powder *3 gm / 1 tsp*
Green chillies *10*
Coriander (*dhaniya*) powder
3 gm / 1 tsp
Mint (*pudina*) *50 gm / ¼ cup*
Green coriander (*hara dhaniya*)
200 gm / 1 cup
Oil for frying

Method

1. Rub the pomfret fillets with salt and malt vinegar.
2. Soak tamarind in hot water and extract pulp.
3. In a blender, make a paste of red chilli powder, green chillies, coriander powder, mint, green coriander and tamarind pulp.
4. Marinate the pomfret fillets in the paste and keep aside for half an hour. Heat oil in a non-stick pan and pan fry the fillets coated with the marinade till crisp.
5. Remove and serve with bread or rice.

SPICY FRIED FISH

Serves: 4-5   Preparation time: 2 hours   Cooking time: 15 minutes

Ingredients

Fish, cut into 5 cm x 5 cm or 2"-
square thin slices *1 kg*
Salt to taste
Lemon juice *25 ml / 5 tsp*
Carom (*ajwain*) seeds *10 gm / 2 tsp*
White pepper (*safed mirch*) powder
8 gm / 1 ²/₃ tsp
Red chilli powder *8 gm / 1 ²/₃ tsp*
Turmeric (*haldi*) powder
8 gm / 1 ²/₃ tsp
Gram flour (*besan*) *120 gm / ²/₃ cup*
Garlic-ginger (*lasan-adrak*) paste
(p. 8) *120 gm / 1 cup*
White vinegar *(sirka) 50 ml / ¹/₄ cup*
Refined oil *500 ml / 2 ¹/₂ cups*
Chaat masala *6 gm / 1 ¹/₃ tsp*

Method

1. Prick fish with a sharp fork.
2. Rub salt and lemon juice over the fish pieces and keep aside for 1-2 hours.
3. Mix all the other ingredients in a bowl except the chaat masala and oil.
4. Dip the fish pieces in the batter and let them stand for another half an hour.
5. Heat the oil in a wok (*kadhai*) and deep fry the fish pieces over medium heat.
6. Sprinkle the fish with chaat masala and serve, accompanied by sliced cucumbers, tomatoes and lemon wedges.

FISH FLAVOURED WITH COCONUT MILK

Serves: 4-5   Preparation time: 10-15 minutes   Cooking time: 30-40 minutes

Ingredients

Fish fillets *600 gm*
Oil *50 ml / 3 ⅔ tbsp*
Green cardamoms *(choti elaichi)* 6
Curry leaves *(meethi neem ke patte)* 2
Green chillies, slit *4-5*
Ginger *(adrak)*, chopped *10 gm / 2 tsp*
Garlic *(lasan)*, chopped *15 gm / 1 tbsp*
Onions, chopped *100 gm / ½ cup*
Turmeric *(haldi)* powder *3 gm / ½ tsp*
Coconut *(nariyal)* milk
500 ml / 2 ½ cups
Salt to taste

Method

1. Heat oil in a wok *(kadhai)*. Add cardamoms, curry leaves, green chillies, ginger and garlic. Stir-fry for a minute. Add onions and sauté till transparent.
2. Stir in turmeric, fish fillets and coconut milk and cook for 15-20 minutes.
3. Season with salt. Bring to a boil and simmer for 8-10 minutes or until the fish is cooked.
4. Transfer to a serving dish and serve hot.

CORIANDER-FLAVOURED POMFRETS

Serves: 4   Preparation time: 20 minutes   Cooking time: 20 minutes

Ingredients

Pomfrets (300-350 gm each) *4*
For the filling:
Green coriander (*hara dhaniya*),
chopped *200 gm / 1 cup*
Green chillies, deseeded, chopped *4*
Ginger (*adrak*) juliennes (long, thin
strips*) 10 gm / 2 tsp*
Garlic (*lasan*), crushed *10 cloves*
Salt
Lemon juice *30 ml / 2 tbsp*
Oil
For the curry:
Yoghurt (*dahi*) (p. 6) *500 gm / 2 ½ cups*
Corriander (*dhaniya*) seeds, broiled,
pounded *60 gm / 4 tbsp*
• Salt
Ginger (*adrak*), chopped *20 gm / 4 tsp*

Coconut (*nariyal*) cream *225 gm / 1 cup*
Onion paste (p. 8) *20 gm / 4 tsp*
Green cardamoms (*choti elaichi*), crushed *5*
Bayleaves (*tej patta*) *4*
Peppercorns, crushed *15 gm / 1 tbsp*
Green chillies, slit *4*
Lemon *1*

Method

1. Clean the pomfrets, debone; make slight slashes.
2. For the filling, mix all the ingredients and smear on the inside and outside of the pomfrets.
3. Heat oil in a pan. Lightly fry the pomfrets on both sides and place on a wide-bottomed oven-proof dish.
4. For the curry, whisk all the ingredients in yoghurt and pour over the fish. Cover and bake for 15 minutes.
5. Serve hot.

PRAWN CURRY

Serves: 4   Preparation time: 45 minutes   Cooking time: 35 minutes

Ingredients

Prawns, cleaned and deveined *1 kg*
Oil *100 ml / ½ cup*
Onion, finely chopped *1*
Garlic *(lasan)*, crushed *5 gm / 1 tsp*
Cloves *(laung)*, ground *5 gm / 1 tsp*
Flour *(maida) 5 gm / 1 tsp*
Turmeric *(haldi)* powder *5 gm / 1 tsp*
Red chilli powder *10 gm / 2 tsp*
Sugar *5 gm / 1 tsp*
Cinnamon *(dalchini)*, ground
5 gm / 1 tsp
Beef or chicken stock *150 ml / ¾ cup*
Creamed coconut *100 gm / ½ cup*
Lemon juice *5 gm / 1 tsp*
Salt to taste

Method

1. Heat oil in a saucepan. Sauté chopped onion, crushed garlic and ground cloves. Fry lightly and add flour, turmeric, chilli powder, sugar and cinnamon. Cook for a few minutes.

2. Gradually add stock and creamed coconut to the pan and bring to a boil, stirring constantly. Reduce heat and simmer for 10 minutes.

3. Add the prawns and lemon juice. Season with salt and cook for another 10 minutes. Serve hot.

MAHI MUSALLAM

(Fish flavoured with cashewnut and fenugreek)

Serves: 4-5   Preparation time: 25 minutes   Cooking time: 1 hour

Ingredients

River or sea fish (whole) *2 kg*
Oil *200 ml / 1 cup*
Onion paste (p. 8) *200 gm / 1 cup*
Ginger (*adrak*) paste (p. 8)
50 gm / ¼ cup
Garlic (*lasan*) paste (p. 8)
50 gm / ¼ cup
Cashewnut (*kaju*) paste
100 gm / ½ cup
Coriander (*dhaniya*) powder
15 gm / 3 tsp
Red chilli powder *10 gm / 2 tsp*
Turmeric (*haldi*) powder *10 gm / 2 tsp*
Salt to taste
Yoghurt (*dahi*) (p. 6) *180 gm / ¾ cup*

Fenugreek (*methi*) powder *6 gm / 1 ⅓ tsp*
Garam masala (p. 6) *15 gm / 3 tsp*
Vetivier (*kewda*) *5 drops*
Lemon juice *15 ml / 1 tbsp*
Green coriander (*hara dhaniya*) *10 gm / 2 tsp*
Butter (*ghee*), melted *30 gm / 2 tbsp*
For the marinade:
Garlic (*lasan*) paste (p. 8) *20 gm / 4 tsp*
Ginger (*adrak*) paste (p. 8) *20 gm / 4 tsp*
Lemon juice *15 ml / 1 tbsp*
Red chilli powder *5 gm / 1 tsp*
Salt to taste

Method

1. Clean, wash and wipe the fish thoroughly.
2. Mix all the ingredients for the marinade. Prick the

fish with a sharp fork, rub the marinade all over and leave aside for an hour.

3. Heat the oil in a pan to smoking point. Arrange the fish in a baking dish. Baste the fish with hot oil.

4. To the oil left in the pan, add onion, ginger-garlic and cashewnut pastes and stir. Add coriander powder, red chilli powder, turmeric powder and salt.

5. Add the yoghurt and bring the mixture to a boil. Reduce to medium heat and stir until the oil separates from the mixture.

6. Add 1 ½ cups hot water and bring the mixture to a slow boil. Add fenugreek powder, garam masala and vetivier.

7. Preheat oven to 120 °C / 250 °F. Pour a portion of the hot gravy over the fish and bake for 40 minutes, basting every 15 minutes with the gravy.

8. Remove the fish and arrange carefully in a shallow dish. Strain the gravy and add the lemon juice. Pour the gravy over the fish and garnish with green coriander and melted butter. Serve with rice.

— ❖ —

Relish Your Pickles

If your pickle jar seems to be getting a fungus layer on top, coat the outside of the jar with salt and mustard oil.

— ❖ —

SHRIMPS WITH MANGOES

Serves: 4   Preparation time: 1 hour 30 minutes   Cooking time: 30 minutes

Ingredients

Shrimps *400 gm*
Turmeric (*haldi*) powder *2 gm / ½ tsp*
Salt to taste
Oil *80 ml / ½ cup*
Mustard (*rai*) seeds *5 gm / 1 tsp*
Curry leaves (*meethi neem
ke patte*) *4*
Onions, chopped *100 gm / ½ cup*
Green chillies, slit *2*
Ginger (*adrak*), chopped
15 gm / 1 tbsp
Garlic (*lasan*), chopped *15 gm / 1 tbsp*
Coriander (*dhaniya*) powder
15 gm / 1 tbsp
Red chilli powder *10 gm / 2 tsp*
Mangoes (*aam*) raw, sliced
200 gm / 1 cup
Coconut (*nariyal*) milk *200 ml / 1 cup*

Method

1. Marinate the shrimps in turmeric powder and salt; keep aside.
2. Heat oil in a wok (*kadhai*). Sauté shrimps. Remove and keep aside.
3. Add mustard seeds and let them crackle.
4. In the same oil, add curry leaves, onions, green chillies, ginger and garlic. Cook till the onions are lightly browned. Add coriander powder and red chilli powder and stir.
5. Mix the shrimps and mangoes into the curry. Add the coconut milk and cook for 15-20 minutes till the curry thickens. Remove from heat.
6. Serve hot.

FISH ROLLS

Serves: 4   Preparation time: 30 minutes   Cooking time: 45 minutes

Ingredients

Fish (2" x 4" strips) *12*
Butter *60 ml / 4 tbsp*
Onions, chopped *4*
Green chillies, slit *3*
Ginger *(adrak)*, chopped *10 gm / 2 tsp*
Turmeric *(haldi)* powder *2 gm / ½ tsp*
Yoghurt *(dahi)* (p. 6), whisked
200 gm / 1 cup
Cream *100 gm / ½ cup*
Fenugreek seeds *(methi dana)*,
broiled, powdered *3 gm / ½ tsp*
Green cardamom *(choti elaichi)*
powder *3 gm / ½ tsp*
Green coriander *(hara dhaniya)*,
chopped *5 gm / 1 tsp*

Method

1. Roll each fish strip and secure with a toothpick.
2. Heat butter in a heavy-bottomed pan and sauté onions until soft.
3. Add green chillies and ginger to the onions and stir-fry for a few minutes.
4. Add turmeric powder, yoghurt, cream, fenugreek seeds and green cardamom powder. Sauté for 10-15 minutes.
5. Place the fish rolls in the sauce and cook on slow fire *(dum)* for 10-15 minutes or until the fish is cooked. Remove from heat.
6. Transfer the fish into a serving dish and remove the toothpicks.
7. Strain the gravy and pour on top of the fish. Serve hot, garnished with green coriander.

FISH IN YOGHURT

Serves: 4   Preparation time: 20 minutes   Cooking time: 25 minutes

Ingredients

Pomfret fillets *700 gm*
Salt to taste
Lemon juice *45 ml / 3 tbsp*
Turmeric (*haldi*) powder *5 gm / 1 tsp*
Oil *100 ml / ½ cup*
Mustard (*rai*) seeds *3 gm / ½ tsp*
Curry leaves (*meethi neem
ke patte*) *10*
Ginger (*adrak*), chopped *20 gm / 4 tsp*
Onions, chopped *75 gm / 5 tbsp*
Tomatoes, chopped *80 gm / 5 ⅔ tbsp*
Red chilli powder *3 gm / ½ tsp*
Cumin (*jeera*) powder *3 gm / ½ tsp*
Coriander (*dhaniya*) powder
3 gm / ½ tsp
Yoghurt (*dahi*) (p. 6), whisked
150 gm / ¾ cup

Method

1. Marinate the pomfret fillets with half the salt, lemon juice and turmeric powder. Keep aside for 15 minutes.
2. Heat oil in a non-stick pan and fry the marinated fillets till they are golden brown. Drain and keep aside.
3. To the same oil, add mustard seeds and curry leaves and sauté till the seeds crackle.
4. Add chopped ginger and onions; cook till onions soften. Add tomatoes and cook till the oil separates.
5. Stir in the red chilli, cumin and coriander powders and the remaining turmeric. Stir for a minute.
6. Mix in yoghurt. Boil and simmer for 7 minutes.
7. Slip the fried fish into the curry and simmer.
8. After four minutes, remove the fillets and place on the serving dish. Pour the curry on top.
9. Serve hot.

COCONUT JHINGA CURRY

(Coconut-flavoured prawn curry)

Serves: 4   Preparation time: 5 minutes   Cooking time: 30 minutes

Ingredients

Prawns (*jhinge*) *1 kg*
Coconut (*nariyal*), grated
75 gm / 5 tbsp
Groundnut oil (*moongphali tel*)
60 ml / 4 tbsp
Mustard (*rai*) seeds *3 gm / 1 tsp*
Onions, chopped *200 gm / 1 cup*
Garlic (*lasan*) paste (p. 8)
20 gm / 4 tsp
Ginger (*adrak*) paste (p. 8)
10 gm / 2 tsp
Coriander (*dhaniya*) powder
10 gm / 2 tsp
Red chilli powder *10 gm / 2 tsp*
Turmeric (*haldi*) powder
3 gm / ½ tsp

Salt to taste
Tomatoes, chopped *300 gm / 1 ½ cups*
Green coriander (*hara dhaniya*), chopped *20 gm / 4 tsp*
Curry leaves *10*

Methods

1. Shell, devein, wash and pat dry the prawns.
2. Blend the coconut with 60 ml / ¼ cup of water and make a fine paste.
3. Heat the oil in a pot *(handi)* and crackle the mustard seeds; then sauté the onions over medium heat till transparent.
4. Add garlic and ginger paste. Stir and cook till the liquid evaporates.
5. Add coriander powder, red chilli powder, turmeric and salt. Stir.

6. Then add the tomatoes and cook till they are mashed.

7. Reduce to low heat, add the coconut paste and the curry leaves. Stir for two minutes.

8. Add the prawns and 1½ cups of water. Bring to a boil, reduce to low heat and simmer, stirring occasionally, until the prawns are cooked.

9. Transfer to a bowl, garnish with coriander and serve hot with boiled rice.

❖

Seasoning Special

When a bottle of chilli sauce is nearly empty, add a little olive oil, vinegar and seasoning to taste. Mix well and use as a salad dressing.

❖

RED SNAPPER MUSSALLAM

(Spicy red snapper)

Serves: 4   Preparation time: 1 hour 30 minutes   Cooking time: 1 hour 30 minutes

Ingredients

Red snapper, whole, cleaned
(700-800 gm each) *2*
For the marinade:
Ginger (*adrak*) paste (p. 8)
5 gm / 1 tsp
Garlic (*lasan*) paste (p. 8)
10 gm / 2 tsp
Salt to taste
Turmeric (*haldi*) powder *3 gm / ½ tsp*
Yoghurt (*dahi*) (p. 6), whisked
250 gm / 1 ⅓ cups
Lemon juice *30 ml / 2 tbsp*
Corriander (*dhaniya*) seeds, roasted,
crushed *10 gm / 2 tsp*
Oil *150 ml / ¾ cup*

For the curry:
Onions, chopped *150 gm / ¾ cup*
Tomatoes, chopped *200 gm / 1 cup*
Coriander (*dhaniya*) powder *15 gm / 1 tbsp*
Red chilli powder *10 gm / 2 tsp*
Cashewnut (*kaju*) paste *15 gm / 1 tbsp*
Garam masala (p. 6) *5 gm / 1 tsp*
Salt to taste
Green coriander (*hara dhaniya*), chopped *20 gm / 4 tsp*

Method

1. Clean the whole fish and make slits on the flesh.
2. Mix together the ingredients for the marinade. Smear evenly on the fish and keep aside for one hour.
3. Heat oil in a wok (*kadhai*) and fry the fish on both sides till golden brown. Remove and keep aside.

4. In the same oil, sauté the chopped onions till transparent. Add the remaining ingredients for the curry, except green coriander.

5. Stir-fry for a few minutes, sprinkling water occasionally.

6. Place the fish in a roasting pan.

7. Pour gravy on top. Cover and cook for 10 minutes.

8. Stir in the remaining marinade; cook and stir for 5 minutes.

9. Place fish in an oven-proof dish; cover and cook for 40 minutes in a moderately hot oven. Serve hot with a green salad.

❖

Anytime Salad!

*If you run out of green vegetables
for salad, mix some finely chopped
onions with boiled chickpeas
(kabuli chana) and serve.*

❖

NOORMEHAL PULAO

(Aromatic rice topped with fried cottage cheese balls)

Serves: 4-5   Preparation time: 45 minutes   Cooking time: 45 minutes

Ingredients

Basmati rice or any long grain variety
400 gm / 2 cups
Refined oil *60 ml / 4 tbsp*
Bayleaf *(tej patta) 1*
Cinnamon *(dalchini)* sticks
(medium) *3*
Cloves *(laung) 6*
Caraway seeds *(shahi jeera)*
3 gm / 2/3 tsp
Green cardamoms *(choti elaichi) 8*
Black pepper *(kali mirch) 10*
Onions, finely chopped *50 gm / 1/4 cup*
Ginger *(lasan)* paste (p. 8)
12 gm / 2 1/2 tsp
Garam masala (p. 6) *10 gm / 2 tsp*

Water / chicken stock *500 ml / 2 1/2 cups*
Salt to taste
Cottage cheese *(paneer)* (p. 8) *100 gm / 1/2 cup*
Cream / milk *50 ml / 3 1/3 tbsp*
Saffron *(kesar)* strands *1 gm / a pinch*
Spinach *(palak)* juice, optional *10 ml / 2 tsp*
Butter *(makhan) 30 gm / 2 tbsp*
Mace *(javitri)* powder *3 gm / 2/3 tsp*
Green coriander *(hara dhaniya)*, chopped *10 gm / 2 tsp*

Method

1. Wash and soak the rice in water for 30 minutes.
2. Heat the oil in a heavy pot; add the bayleaf, cinnamon, cloves, caraway seeds, cardamoms and black pepper. Sauté over medium heat till the spices begin to crackle.

3. Add onions; stir and cook till soft and golden. Add ginger paste and garam masala and sauté for 30-40 seconds.

4. Add the rice, stir and cook over medium heat for 3-4 minutes. Add water / chicken stock, bring a boil and add salt. Lower the heat, cover and cook till the rice is done and the liquid has evaporated.

5. While the rice is cooking, grate the cottage cheese in a bowl. Mix in 10 ml of cream / milk and season with salt. Divide this mixture into three portions. Mix one portion with the saffron dissolved in 10 ml of cream / milk and the second portion with the spinach juice; keep the third portion as it is.

6. Make small balls of 4-5 gm each from these mixtures and fry them in butter. (These balls are called the Noormehal.)

7. Add mace powder to the remaining cream / milk and keep aside.

8. Transfer the pulao to a serving platter. Garnish with the cottage cheese balls, green coriander and lace with cream / milk mixture. Serve hot.

———— ❖ ————

Add a 'Meaty' Flavour

To prepare vegetable biryani with a 'meaty flavour,' add a little lemon grass while cooking it.

———— ❖ ————

PARDA CHILMAN BIRYANI

(Mutton biryani coated with a pastry)

Serves: 4-5   Preparation time: 50 minutes   Cooking time: 1 hour

Ingredients

Lamb chops on a single bone *1 kg*
Basmati rice or any long grain
variety *600 gm / 3 cups*
Saffron *(kesar) ½ gm / a pinch*
Milk *30 ml / 2 tbsp*
Cream *50 gm / ¼ cup*
Vetivier *(kewda) 3 drops*
Yoghurt *(dahi)* (p. 6) *300 gm / 1 ½ cups*
Mint *(pudina)* leaves *10 gm / 2 tsp*
Green coriander *(hara dhaniya)*
10 gm / 2 tsp
Water / lamb stock *200 ml / 1 cup*
Bayleaves *(tej patta) 2*
Cinnamon *(dalchini)* sticks *2*
Green cardamoms *(choti elaichi) 10*
Cloves *(laung) 10*

Salt to taste, Oil *50 ml / ¼ cup*
Caraway seeds *(shahi jeera) 6 gm / 1 ⅓ tsp*
Onion paste (p. 8) *100 gm / ½ cup*
Ginger-garlic *(adrak-lasan)* paste (p. 8) *100 gm / ½ cup*
Garlic *(lasan)* paste (p. 8) *45 gm / 3 tbsp*
Red chillies *6*
Yellow chilli powder *(deghi mirch) 10 gm / 2 tsp*
Mace *(javitri)* powder *3 gm / ⅔ tsp*
Onions, sliced, fried *50 gm / ¼ cup*
Lemon juice *5 gm / 1 tsp*
Butter *(makhan)*, unsalted *200 gm / 1 cup*
Flour *(maida) 600 gm / 3 cups*
Eggs, beaten *2*

Method

1. Wash the rice and soak for 30 minutes.
2. Whisk yoghurt in a bowl and divide into two equal

portions. Dissolve saffron in milk and cream. Add vetivier drops, mint, green coriander and one portion of yoghurt to this.

3. Preheat the oven to 150 °C / 300 °F.

4. Boil 4 lt of water in a saucepan and add a bayleaf, a cinnamon stick, 2 green cardamoms, 2 cloves and salt to taste. Add the rice and boil until it is half done. Drain the rice with the whole spices and keep hot.

5. Heat the oil in another saucepan; add the remaining whole spices and caraway seeds and sauté over medium heat. Add the onion paste and sauté until golden brown. Add the ginger and garlic pastes, red chillies and yellow chilli powder and stir for 15 seconds.

6. Stir in the lamb chops and salt and cook for a further 3-4 minutes. Add a portion of the plain yoghurt and approximately 200 ml of water. Stir and bring to a boil. Lower the heat and simmer until the chops are done.

7. To assemble the biryani, grease a baking dish. Spread half the lamb-mixture, sprinkle half the saffron / yoghurt / mint / coriander mixture and top with half the parboiled rice. Repeat the process until the prepared mixtures are used up. Sprinkle mace powder, fried onions and lemon juice.

8. Mix the butter into the flour; add one egg and enough milk to make a stiff dough. Roll out the dough and cover the rice and lamb mixture with it. Seal the edges and brush with the other beaten egg. Slow-bake in an oven *(dum)* for 10-15 minutes. Serve hot.

PUDINA PARANTHA

(Wholewheat bread flavoured with mint)

Serves: 4   Preparation time: 30 minutes   Cooking time: 10 minutes

Ingredients

Wholewheat flour (*atta*)
½ kg / 2 ½ cups
Salt *5 gm / 1 tsp*
Clarified butter (*ghee*)
120 gm / ½ cup
Water *250 ml / 1 ¼ cups*
Mint (*pudina*) leaves, dried
5 gm / 1 tsp

Method

1. Mix flour, salt and half of clarified butter; add water and knead to a smooth dough. Cover and keep aside for 30 minutes.

3. Shape the dough into a ball. Flatten into a round disc with a rolling pin. Apply the remaining clarified butter and sprinkle dried mint leaves.

4. Pleat the dough into 1 collected strip. Shape into balls and roll out into 6"-diameter pancakes.

5. Heat a griddle (*tawa*)/tandoor and cook till brown spots appear on both the sides.

Taftan

Khasta Roti

Pudina Parantha

Missi Roti

TAFTAN

(Rich, leavened, rice-flour bread)

Serves: 4   Preparation time: 1 hour
Cooking time: 10 minutes

Ingredients

Rice flour (*chawal ka atta*) 480 gm / 2 ½ cups
Salt to taste, Water
Sugar *3 gm / ½ tsp*
Milk *240 ml / 1 cup*
Clarified butter *(ghee) 180 gm / ³/₄ cup*
Yeast *3 gm / ½ tsp*
Melon *(magaz) seeds 10 gm / 2 tsp*
Green coriander (*hara dhaniya*),
chopped *10 gm / 2 tsp*

Method

1. Sieve flour and salt together.
2. Make a well in the flour. Add water, sugar, milk, clarified butter, yeast and melon seeds. Mix gradually and knead into a soft dough.
3. Divide into 4 equal balls and set aside for half an hour.
4. Dust lightly and roll into 3 ½" discs, ¼" thick. Sprinkle with coriander.
5. Bake in a tandoor till brown.
6. Brush with clarified butter and serve hot.

MISSI ROTI

(Flavoured gram-flour bread cooked in a tandoor)

Serves: 4   Preparation time: 30 minutes
Cooking time: 10 minutes

Ingredients

Gram flour (*besan*) *300 gm / 1 ½ cups*
Flour (*maida*) *100 gm / ½ cup*
Green chillies, chopped *25 gm / 5 tsp*
Ginger (*adrak*), chopped *25 gm / 5 tsp*

Green coriander (*hara dhaniya*),
chopped *25 gm / 5 tsp*
Pomegranate seeds (*anardana*), *20 gm / 4 tsp*
Cumin (*jeera*) seeds *15 gm / 1 tbsp*
Onion seeds (*kalonji*) *25 gm / 5 tsp*
Salt *10 gm / 2 tsp*
Butter *100 gm / ½ cup*
Clarified butter (*ghee*) *30 gm / 2 tbsp*

Method

1. Chop green chillies, ginger and coriander finely.

2. Crush pomegranate, cumin and onion seeds with a rolling pin.

3. Mix all ingredients except butter; knead to a soft dough with water.

4. Shape into balls and roll out into 6"-diameter pancakes.

5. Cook on a griddle (*tawa*) or in a tandoor until brown on both sides.

6. Remove from fire, apply butter and serve hot.

KHASTA ROTI

(Wholewheat oven-baked bread)

Serves: 4-5   Preparation time: 25 minutes   Cooking time: 10-15 minutes

Ingredients

Wholewheat flour (*atta*) *500 gm / 2½ cups*
Salt to taste, Sugar *12 gm / 2½ tsp*
Carom (*ajwain*) seeds *15 gm / 1 tbsp*
Water *300 ml / 1½ cups*

Method

1. Sieve flour; add salt, sugar and carom seeds. Knead into a hard dough with water. Cover with a moist cloth and keep aside for 15 minutes.

2. Divide the dough into 10 balls. Dust and roll into 10 cm *rotis*. Prick with a fork evenly.

3. Bake the *rotis* in an oven at 175 °C / 350 °F for 8-10 minutes or till light brown in colour.

Glossary of Cooking Terms

Baste: Moisten meat, poultry or game during roasting by spooning over it, its juices.

Broil: Cook on a rack or on a gridiron.

Blanch: Immerse in boiling water so that the peel comes off.

Devein: Remove the main central vein from a fish.

Fillet: The undercut of a loin or ribs of meat, boned sides of fish or boned breasts of poultry.

Garnish: Decorate with lemon wedges, tomato slices, etc. to improve the appearance and flavour.

Marinade: A seasoned mixture of oil, vinegar, lemon juice, etc. in which meat, poultry and fish is left for some time to soften its fibres and add flavour to it.

Roast: Cook in an oven or in open heat.

Sauté: Fry quickly over strong heat in fat or oil.

Simmer: Keep boiling gently on low heat.

Skewer: Fasten together pieces of food compactly on a specially designed long pin, for cooking.

Stir-fry: Fry rapidly while stirring and tossing.

Whisk: To beat air rapidly into a mixture with an egg beater, rotary beater or electric beater.

INDEX

STARTERS

DRY DISHES

CURRIES

ACCOMPANIMENTS

ACKNOWLEDGEMENTS

Grateful thanks to the Master Chefs at **The Intercontinental Hotel,** New Delhi, and the **Oberoi Group of Hotels,** New Delhi, for making available their kitchens for the preparation and photography of the dishes.

ISBN: 978-81-7436-074-8

Fourth impression 2007
© **Roli & Janssen BV**
Published in India by Roli Books in arrangement with Roli & Janssen BV
M 75, Greater Kailash II Market, New Delhi-110 048, INDIA
Tel.: (011) 29212271, 29212782, Fax: (011) 29217185
E-mail: roli@vsnl.com, Website: rolibooks.com

Photographs: Dheeraj Paul

Printed in Singapore